POEMS FOR THE REDEEMED HEART

K.A. BECHTEL

Poems for the Redeemed Heart

K. A. Bechtel

Storybunk.com

ISBN: 978-0-578-66135-3

Printed in the United States of America

APPRECIATION:

To Tirus Twyne and Nick Seek, my dearest brothers in Christ and mighty warriors in the faith. You both have helped me grow to in godliness in so many ways!

…

To Pastor David Brandt, who has taught me and many others God's word as a teenager and has greatly encouraged me to make this book a reality!

…

To Ralph Bechtel, a faithful servant of the Gospel whom God has used to stir into me a deep love of Jesus when I was a child. You are also a wonderful Uncle!

...

To Betty Herb, who is an encouragement to all in our church and who was kind enough to edit this book by noting my many grammar mistakes!

...

To the Lebanon Bible Fellowship Church, for teaching me the scriptures at a young age and letting me use my gifts in many ways! Most of all, I hope this book is an encouragement to all of you, and a testament to how preaching the Bible can affect the lives of the young!

TABLE OF CONTENTS

INTRODUCTION 1

SECTION ONE: JESUS 11

JESUS THROUGH THE EYES OF… 15

POEMS FOR CHRISTMAS...27

    IMMANUEL! GOD WITH US!................................28

    THE GLORY IN THE MANGER............................30

    HOPE IN THE MANGER.......................................32

    AN ALTERNATIVE ENDING TO THE HYMN *O'*
    COME O' COME EMMANUEL.................................33

POEMS ON THE DEATH AND RESURRECTION: 35

    BLOOD ON THE DOORPOST 36

    MY SAVIOR HUNG UPON A TREE 40

    THE BODY ON THE TREE 42

    LOVE IS A NAIL..43

    WOODEN CROSS, FOR THE LOST.....................44

    TOMB OPENED 46

    THE GOSPEL IN 5 STANZAS. 47

    IT IS FINISHED 49

    HIS RIGHTEOUSNESS...51

    GIVE ME THE CROSS..55

    CHRIST DIED FOR THE UNGODLY.....................56

POEMS IN AWE OF JESUS 59

    OH, TO SEE THE FACE OF JESUS..........................60

    THERE IS NO OTHER POWER I'LL TRUST..........61

    POETIC GLEANINGS ON THE NAME OF JESUS ..63

POEM ON THE WORD..65

MY VEIL WAS LIFTED, NOW I SEE 67

SECTION: SIN 70

WHAT I AM IN CHRIST, I AM NOT. SO I SAY:.....73

BACKSLIDE 77

INTRODUCTION: 79

TEAR DOWN YOUR IDOLS...................................79

WHERE IS MY GOD?..86

TREASURES...88

LADY LUST 90

OH, THE DAY WHEN ALL SIN IS NO MORE 96

MASTER OF KINDNESS 98

YET HE LOVES ME SO! 99

GIVE US GRACE 101

SECTION: HOPE AND LONGING 104

EVERY LONGING OF MINE...................................107

WHEN MY HEART FEELS GLOOMY...................110

GLEANINGS ON SADNESS 112

WHATEVER GAIN THIS WORLD MAY HAVE ...113

HAVE FAITH IN THE FAITHFUL 114

HOPE REFOCUSED...116

HOPE IN THE LORD 118

THERE IS A CITY, NOT FAR AWAY....................119

CITY MADE BY GOD 120

SECTION: LIFE OF WORSHIP 125

A LOVE THAT REACHES 127

WORTHSHIP 128

"WE" 129

WE LIVE 130

JOY AMIDST THE FLAMES 131

MAY I TAKE UP MY CROSS AND FOLLOW THEE
.... 133

LORD, I AM YOUR SERVENT.............................. 135

STOP WAITING, SINGLE SOUL: 136

LIKE A TREE, STANDS THE MAN 143

EARS TO LISTEN 144

CONFORM ME TO CHRIST 145

GIVE THANKS IN ALL THINGS 146

DIVINE INTERJECTION 148

SECTION: OUR BIG GOD.................................... 150

TRINITARIAN POETRY JAM 153

KING OF KINGS, TO YOU WE SING! 154

CREATED BY GOD TO WORSHIP HIM................ 155

THE POT AND THE CREATOR 157

ALL WILL KNOW THAT YOU ARE GOD 159

AWAKEN OUR HEARTS.. 161

A HYMN ON GOD'S CHOICE.............................. 163

SECTION: BONUS FEATURES 166

WINTER IN THE SPRING................................. 168

TACOS 169

I PAINT PICTURES WITH MY WORDS 171

SNEAK PEAK:.. 174

ABOUT THE AUTHOR 177

INTRODUCTION

I don't remember my first poem. It might be in here, but I don't know. Let's be honest though, it probably isn't. Like every art form, poetry must be practiced in order to grow. I've practiced poetry a lot. Ever since middle school and high school the written word has been my favorite mode of self-expression. I don't know why; perhaps it developed because I wasn't too good at showing people what was really inside my heart.

Now I am not saying that I'm not a vocal or self-expressive person or that I'm not good at "putting on a smile." I truly believe that a cheerful heart is good medicine. Unfortunately, though sometimes I forget that having a cheerful heart doesn't mean you always have to smile or hide the struggles in your life, being a Christian didn't mean I had to be happier than everyone else. It meant that I knew the source of life better than most of my peers. You can know the source of life and still have problems. Just ask the Psalmists!

This "source of life" has somehow inevitably been the primary subject of my poems. When it comes to any other type of writing I usually choose fiction. I've always had a creative mind filled with stories as a kid. But when it came to poetry, I just couldn't stop writing about the source of life. This is no fictional story; this is something I believe with all my heart. Some people write poems about lost love, beautiful sunsets, how awesome their life is, or even about their cats, but, to me, there is no greater or more beautiful subject than that of my wonderful savior, Jesus Christ.

You might have realized by now that I am not trying to have a "professional" tone. I rather decided to write my introduction in a more conversational manner. I'm not here to drown you in theological debates or theories, though such books are valuable: simply put, I want to offer this book to you as a simple Christian who wants to see his brothers and sisters (as well as anyone interested in joining our merry band of Christ-lovers) a number of poems to lead each other to greater worship of our Lord!

Ultimately, Jesus is subject of this little book, so perhaps some background on my own faith journey and a basic understanding of my faith is in order. I became a Christian at a young age. I wish I knew the exact age or date, but I don't. All I know is that Jesus completely changed my life. This Jesus guy promised to be a friend unlike any other, but, more than that, he promised to save me from my sin. I want to clarify what sin is. You will hear about sin all throughout this little book because it's the reason Jesus came to earth. Sin is rebellion against God; it's doing what we want no matter what, despite the bad consequences. Ultimately, sin is not loving God and not loving your neighbor. Sin is bad; God is good. God must punish sin; and sin brings God's just wrath upon me. So, I had a problem.

I know it's not always socially acceptable to talk about God as a wrathful God. No one wants to sound like one of those churches that pickets funerals with demeaning "God hates you" signs. That's why it's so important to understand who God is as a whole and to not just accept certain parts of him. If sin is so bad and God is so good, if God is the judge, and we are his rebellious creatures, then he has every right to send us to Hell. It's a sobering fact, but true. If we truly believe in a good God, then we must realize that he must punish sin. Every wrong done to us, and everything we do wrong to others will be judged justly. But often, those in false churches fail to see the whole picture of God, for he is also a God of love.

That's why I love Jesus so much. If you're not a Christian, you gotta see things through my worldview here. If I am convinced that I am such a bad sinner in need of grace, and I believe that this guy named Jesus came a long time ago to give me more grace and mercy than I could possibly imagine, then it makes perfect sense for me to be so obsessed with Jesus. I believe Jesus is God. I believe God the Father sent Jesus (who is God the Son) to live a perfect life that I could not live and to die in my place. Jesus was not only fully God, but also fully Man. He took on human flesh and voluntarily bore the wrath of God for me. He took God's anger so that I could bear God's undeserved yet never-ending love and grace. Then Jesus gave me his righteousness (or goodness) so that in the eyes of God the Father I could be seen as perfect and pure. Jesus died on a Roman cross for my sin… but then he rose again bodily from the grave saying that whoever believes in him and trusts in him alone for salvation can be part of God's family and have eternal life. And, if Jesus really did rise from the grave, I can be sure that I am not deceived! So, you can see why Jesus makes me so excited; because of him I can know God now and will experience eternity with him. My mere words are not adequate to describe these glories to you. If you want a better explanation of who he is, I suggest reading the four Gospels.

If you don't know Jesus as your Savior, please be aware that I did not primarily put this book together just for you. But I do hope that it would not only be an enjoyable read for you, but also one that might challenge you. I pray that through it you might come to know Jesus or at least be more open to knowing about him. I made this book for my fellow Christian brothers and sisters to be able to read and encourage themselves with. May these poems be a bright reminder of the God who is love! So, I do encourage anyone who is not a Christ-follower and may have picked up this book to keep reading. Perhaps seeing how Jesus changed my heart (and still is changing my heart) will grow your interest in he who truly is "Life."

I have written these for Redeemed Hearts - those who have been brought out of slavery to sin and have been freed to serve the one true and loving God! In the Bible to be redeemed means to be purchased from one thing to another thing. At times it's been used to describe the purchase of property or of a slave. For instance, the book of Exodus says the Israelites, who were being oppressed by their earthly masters in Egypt, were brought out of Egypt to serve a new master, God (Deuteronomy 4:20). In a similar way, those who believe in Jesus were brought out of slavery to sin to be a joyful slave to our righteous God (Romans 6:17-18). That might not sound nice in our culture, and I want to recognize that. We've seen in the last few centuries some of the most horrific acts done in slavery. Even the slavery in the New Testament time (the 1st Century) was not as good as many people defend it to be. But the authors of the New Testament (and of the Old) saw an important concept in it that they didn't want anyone to miss. We are all a slave to something. We all have a Master. And it's either sin or God. One leads to death, but the other leads to life. We were made to worship God, so let us choose God.

Now you might be discouraged because you have believed in Jesus and you are trying to obey God, but you keep failing. My friend, we will fail, A LOT! But God's grace not only covers our sin but also helps us to overcome our sins! When you fail, ask God for help, but also ask his community (the Church) and see what God might do. It isn't always easy, but he loves you dearly and wants you to be more like him! That's what he's predestined us for after all, to be made like Jesus. While in this present life we may struggle to obey, one day when God calls us home, we will be perfect like him. But in this life, it still can be a struggle.

In the following pages you'll see a lot of that. To be honest, most of these poems I never planned on sharing. There have been a select few that I've shared with friends, but I never really planned on publishing half of them. Nevertheless, God's been showing me some new and exciting ways to use my gifts and talents. Recently I've took my first step into the world of self-publishing with my first book and short story, "Mud & Daisies." I've created a blog, Storybunk.com, to promote the things I write. But I have also started asking myself the question many people at my church and at my college have asked me before: "Why don't you publish your poems?" I always told them that I don't have enough yet or I don't know how. But now I think I do, as evidenced by the existence of this book.

This little book is a collection of poems I wrote over the past eight years. Some have been slightly edited to be more universally applicable, while others have been kept "raw" to be a testimony of God's work in my life. And if God can work in my life, I know he wants to work in yours, too.

I want to add one final note. If you are looking for a super professional poetry book, this isn't it. This is more of your laid back, "Ooo that sounds interesting" type of poetry book. You can complain about the stanzas if you want, but I rarely worry about the stanzas. I typically go for sound and content, and at times I find they're almost lyrical. My goal is that, if my poems were ever to be put to song, they would be theologically rich and edifying to those singing them. With that said, I am no song writer, so I don't have any plans to "songify" any of them, but I do want to share them with you, my fellow brothers and sisters in Christ, because I believe God can use them to edify and encourage you as well as point your mind back to the Scriptures!

And that really is the goal of this book - to edify and encourage you and to ultimately; exalt Jesus. I offer this book to Jesus to use as he pleases, and I pray that those reading might be led to greater rejoicing in him who loves them with an everlasting love.

SECTION ONE: JESUS

No one ever encountered Jesus and came out unchanged. The Apostle Paul, upon seeing Jesus on the road to Damascus was transformed from the inside out; he left his life of persecuting Christians and turned to bring more people to Christ than many of us ever will. And the Pharisees who heard Jesus time and time again wouldn't remain unchanged either, except they didn't have such a noble outcome. They sought to put him to death because he claimed to be God (John 8:56-59).

Jesus truly is unlike any other man in history. John 1:14 says that *"Word became flesh and dwelt among us."* In other words, Jesus is God in the flesh. The Bible teaches that Jesus is fully God and fully man and tells us that God came to dwell with us. You see, Jesus came to solve the greatest problem we have - separation from God. Our sin has caused such a great rift in our relationships not only with each other, but also between us and God. This rift was so great that no one except God himself could fix it. And that is what Jesus came to do. He came to fix the rift by willingly bearing our punishment on the cross. My poem *His Righteousness* speaks of this amazing truth. Because of Jesus I am no longer under God's wrath but under his grace! I've been made alive in Christ (Ephesians 2:1-7). I'm a friend of God! "But wait," you might say. "What's the use of a dead savior?" Well, Spoiler Alert! Jesus rose again bodily from the grave proving that he alone is God and can save.

This is perhaps the greatest difference between Christianity and all other religions. Religion teaches that we must do something to get to God: go to church, do good deeds, etc. Christianity teaches something entirely different. Christianity teaches that Jesus came down to bring us to the Father. It's God's work, not ours. Jesus died for our sin, he bore God's wrath, and he can make us a part of God's family.

Christianity is all about grace, but, even more importantly, Christianity is all about Jesus!

And so, I've designed this section to speak about different aspects of Jesus. First we shall start by looking at his birth and then reflecting on his Death and Resurrection. You may find that these tend to overlap, but that's the point. When I talk about Jesus, I want to talk about everything! I want to realize who he is, what he has done, and why it's important. The last part of this section I've entitled "In Awe of Jesus." If Jesus truly is God (and he is) then he is to be worshiped and praised. He should be the very theme of our lives. Please join with me in worshiping my King!

JESUS THROUGH THE EYES OF…

It doesn't take much insight to realize that when people think of Jesus there are a lot of opinions about who exactly he is. In fact, even in Jesus' day people wondered the same thing. You need to look no further than Matthew 16:13-16 to see that even as Jesus walked the earth there were many opinions on who he was. Was he a prophet? Or was he much more? Simon Peter said, "You are the Christ!"

But not everyone agreed with Peter and the disciples; the Pharisees and others said that Jesus was demon possessed (Matthew 10:19-20), still others came to Jesus only to have their physical needs met (like the crowd in John 6). So, who is Jesus? Who is the Christ? Matthew 17:5 holds the key, "This is my beloved Son, with whom I am well pleased, listen to him." If you want to know who Jesus is, obey the Father and listen to him.

Yet still there are many views of who Jesus is. The intent of this poem is to paint a picture of how common day people thought of Jesus during his ministry and to show who he actually is! May you be edified by this poem and may your heart be stirred with affection towards the Son of God!

So now, let's look at Jesus through the eyes of...

The Pharisees

Who does this man think he is
To speak against our laws,
To call us vipers, hypocrites
On whom God's wrath will fall?
Does he not know who we are?
We're teachers of God's Law!
He only says, "listen to them,
But be not like them at all!"

Maybe he has a demon,
Maybe he's Satan's spawn?
Yet still he keeps proclaiming
That he will fulfil the Law.
He claims to come from God above
And blasphemes God's pure name,
And says we will not see God
If we don't believe HIS name!

Who ever thought a man like this

Would talk to sinners so;

He reaches out to the unclean

And makes their bodies whole.

The Pharisees say he's a fraud

And say that he's possessed,

But how can demons raise the dead

And give the weary rest?

I do not know who he may be,

But this one thing I know,

He welcomes the low and despised,

So to him we will go.

To see the captive's bonds released

As sick men's lives are healed,

God's kingdom has been brought to earth.

He wipes away our tears!

The Disciples

We know that he's much more than this;

We know he's more than man.

He claims to come from God above

And forgives sinful man.

He teaches us, but there's much more

That we think he has planned;

For we know he's the Christ of God

Who's come to save this land!

Yet where's his army; where's his sword?

The Romans are still here.

He says to love your neighbor

And tells us "do not fear."

Be we just can't shake this feeling

That he's got more in store;

He speaks of crucifixion

And says his death is sure.

The Romans

Why did they bring this man to us?

What danger could he be?

They say to put him on a cross

Because of blasphemy.

They say he's against Caesar.

They say that he's a king,

Though he led no rebellion.

What trouble could he bring?

He claims to give life to all man;

He claims to save the world,

But now that he's upon a cross

His failure is assured.

People laugh as they walk by,

As their king was lifted high,

And so the innocent man died

With a God forsaken cry.

The Demons

We tried to tempt him in the flesh

But he would not give in.

We knew that he would never sin,

So we would just kill him.

The time to strike the heel had come,

To destroy Adam's Seed,

We laughed with hate, cursing God

As we did the deed.

Our prince knew that the end would come.

Our plans would soon unfurl,

For still God ruled over all things

And planned to save the world.

But we don't care, we'll spread more lies

For that is what we do,

Even though our plan may fail

After a day or two… Or three.

But I sent him with purpose

To die a sinner's death,

So that those who would trust in him

Might have eternal rest.

He did what no other man could

And fulfilled all my laws;

He was the perfect sacrifice

To reverse Adam's fall.

I sent him to reveal myself,

And show that God loved man,

And show that there's forgiveness

In the Son of Man.

My Christ came from the promised seed,

And in faithfulness he bore

All the filthy sins of man

So they bear them no more.

And I shall glorify my Son,

And raise him from the dead,

And give him all authority

For for the world he bled.

And at his name all knees will bow

And give eternal praise,

For through him, and through him alone,

My people will be saved!

And now we do not stand condemned,

But can approach our God,

For he's given us righteousness,

And in light now we trod.

Nothing could ever separate

Us from his mercy great,

We know we could not earn this gift,

That's why we call it grace.

And so we sing with outstretched hands

And glorify his name,

For he has given us new life,

His people whom he saved!

We are The Church, we are his Bride,

He is our Friend and by our side;

But best of all he is our God.

To Jesus be all praise!

POEMS FOR CHRISTMAS

IMMANUEL! GOD WITH US!

Long before time began, God did have a perfect plan,

A plan to save and to redeem those with vile and wicked schemes.

For when the time had fully come, God the Father sent his Son;

The Great I AM came down to us to save us from our sinful lusts.

Born in a manger full of hay; with beasts of burdens he did lay,

God the Son became flesh that day, and only shepherds came his way.

But soon the wise men came around, following the star till him they found,

The one who would die for their sin and three days later rise again.

This child would live a sinless life; this Jesus came to give us light.

He came to save us from God's wrath, to give us peace on earth at last!

And now he is the triumphant one, who forgave us of the evil we've done;

He sent the Spirit to open our eyes and change us from the inside.

So this Christmas don't forget, him who truly paid your debt;

In him we must always trust. Immanuel! God with us!

THE GLORY IN THE MANGER

The glory in the manger,

His glory in the bed,

Where beasts of burdens breed

The Savior lays his head.

The high and lofty glorious

Who took on human flesh

To save us from our troubles

And give eternal rest.

The glory from the highest

Has come down here to earth,

The glory that came to us

In a lowly Virgin's birth.

His glory shown to sinful man,

The holy God most high.

He came to earth to free us;

He came to earth to die.

The glory walked among us;

His glory he did share,

Though he was high and holy,

In love he always cared.

His brow was filled with thorns

His side pierced with a spear,

The Glory of the highest

Died with a mournful tear.

Yet his Glory could not die,

For in Glory he was raised,

As they touched his nail pierced hands,

To the Father they gave praise.

Still his glory shines amongst us,

As we follow in his way.

He is never to depart us,

To him glory, to him praise!

HOPE IN THE MANGER

There is hope in the manger.

There is hope in the hay.

There is hope where the little, silent boy lay.

There is peace everlasting.

There is love untold.

For the child who sleeps,

The whole universe he holds.

AN ALTERNATIVE ENDING TO THE HYMN
O' COME O' COME EMMANUEL.
(Because I can)

"He came, he came, Emmanuel,

To rescue captive Israel.

He shed his blood for all who believe,

And rose again to reign eternally!

Rejoice, Rejoice, Emmanuel.

Has come to thee, O Israel!"

POEMS ON THE DEATH AND RESURRECTION:

INTRODUCTION:
BLOOD ON THE DOORPOST

Jesus is our Passover Lamb! In order to truly understand why the scripture refers to Jesus as "the lamb of God" we must understand the system God put in place for Israel when they violated God's Law. When someone sinned, they'd have to offer a sacrifice, which was usually a spotless lamb. It was blood for blood. The lamb would die in place of the person or assembly. And, boy, would that be a lot of lambs!

Before exiting Egypt, the Israelites were told to slaughter a spotless year-old lamb and spread its blood around their doorposts in order to escape the final plague in Egypt: the death of the firstborn sons. They obeyed God, and when the angel of death came in Exodus 12, we see the Israelites spared and even ready to go on an exodus into the promised land. All of this, of course, was a symbol of something greater to come.

Jesus is our spotless lamb who died in our place. In Jesus, God's just wrath passes over us and is poured onto him. May we proclaim with John the Baptizer, "Behold the Lamb of God, who takes away the sins of the word" (John 1:29)! There is Blood on the Doorposts… Jesus was slain so that God's wrath would "Pass-over" us!

BLOOD ON THE DOORPOSTS

The Blood on the doorposts, The Lamb on the Cross
To break the bonds of slavery and rescue now the lost.

His wrath went around us, his anger passed us by,
For on his Son his anger fell, his wrath is satisfied.

The Blood on the doorposts, The Lamb on the Cross
To break the bonds of slavery and rescue now the lost.

Our chains would not loosen till nails pierced his hands,
When out of death we finally came, in freedom we now stand.

The Blood on the doorposts, The Lamb on the Cross
To break the bonds of slavery and rescue now the lost.

And into his kingdom and to that promised land,
We work on earth until he comes and praise the living Lamb!

The Blood on the doorpost, The Lamb on the Cross,

He was the perfect sacrifice, and finally death has lost!

MY SAVIOR HUNG UPON A TREE

My savior hung upon a tree
Where he bled and died for me.
And in his death the God-Man died;
"It is finished! was his cry.

Light of the World in darkness hung;
The righteous one no longer sung.
For life had died, and in the tomb,
Our faith and hope, it all seems doomed!

Dead as can be, oh, don't you see
The one who promised to save me?
That is until day number three!
The stone is gone; where could he be?

"He is not here," The angels say
And many saw him on that day.
"He is Risen," was their cry!
And so he gives eternal life!

My savior reigns eternally,

For he died and rose to save poor me,

And he'll come back one day, you'll see!

The Risen King! I welcome thee!

THE BODY ON THE TREE

The body on the tree,

The Lamb who died for me.

By death my death has died,

My debt is satisfied.

The thorns upon his head,

In darkness there he bled.

Condemned and crucified,

God's wrath now pacified.

Now sick and soiled me,

Is righteous and now free!

LOVE IS A NAIL

Love is a nail piercing through the flesh.

Love is the blood running down the brow.

Love is a whip tearing away the skin piece by piece.

Love is willingly being crushed in place of your enemy.

Love is hanging naked on a cross so that others might be clothed.

Love is being spat on and mocked, but not retaliating.

Love is letting your life be ruined so that someone else's might be transformed.

Love is being able to escape, but refusing, so that others might escape.

Love is a lamb slaughtered so that sin might be forgiven.

Love is a dead man hanging upon a cross.

Love is God dying for man.

Love is Jesus.

And if you know him, love is in you.

Let us love like him.

WOODEN CROSS, FOR THE LOST

Blood stained, sin's pain,
How the spotless lamb was slain!

Death's price, hate's vice,
Jesus died to give us life.

Wooden cross, for the lost
This is what our sin does cost.

Crown of thorns, he adorned
Our Holy God was met with scorn.

Mocking crowds, shouting loud
Yet he forgave their evil howl.

"It is finished," he proclaimed,
Proving blood covers our stain.

Immanuel died, he paid our price
To give true and undeserved life.

Death defeated, he rose again,

Bringing life to lifeless men!

Only God, The Three in One

Cleans the hearts of those he won.

Forgave our sins, changed our minds.

This God I know, Forever mine!

TOMB OPENED

We had no hope of freedom,

We had no hope of peace,

Until the stone was rolled away,

Now hope will never cease.

For from that tomb came righteousness,

For from it came out life.

And from his mercy pure and good

Emerged such wondrous light.

If he would have stayed there,

Dead forever more,

Never would we have this hope

That is so true and sure.

People search for answers,

But they don't look to him,

But we will look to Christ our lord

And fully trust in him.

THE GOSPEL IN 5 STANZAS.

When deeds of darkness wore us down,
And in God's wrath we would be bound,
His love quickly came crashing down,
When in Christ Jesus we were found!

He bore our curse upon a tree;
He did all of this for you and me;
He makes the dead man finally breathe
And is with us eternally.

He rose again up from the grave,
Proving that only he can save.
His Righteousness is ours today,
For Christ the Lord has made a way!

And now he's at the Father' side,
And in his power, we can hide;
For our King now reigns on high
And watches o'er us day and night.

Sin is not here to stay;

"His Spirit cleansed us" we can say,

And He still works in us today,

For we'll be like Jesus one day!

IT IS FINISHED

It is finished;

Death has lost,

For on that tree he paid the cost.

My debt was great;

His grace was more,

And on that tree my sins he bore.

He nailed them to that cursed tree

To purchase redemption for me.

It is finished;

All is done;

Redemption's story has been sung

To bring dead men back to life

By his perfect sacrifice,

Which has purchased sickened souls

To bring them into glory.

It is finished;

This is true.

Indeed, there is no more to do.

No works of mine could ever bear

The weight of sin that he bore there.

He rose alive up from the grave;

Glory to the one who saves!

INTRODUCTION:
HIS RIGHTEOUSNESS

I still remember when I wrote this. I was at a training camp with my uncle on teaching children the gospel, and I was supposed to be working on a Bible lesson. You may have guessed that I became side-tracked. I did get the lesson done, but all I wanted to talk about at that moment was the righteousness that we have in Jesus Christ. I didn't think that was an easy subject to talk about to kids.

But why not? You don't even have to use the word righteousness (at least right away). I mean, it's simple: Jesus was perfect. We are not. But when Jesus died on the cross, he was called a sinner, so that we could be called righteous or perfect in God's eyes. God took off the dirty old clothes of sin and clothed us with Jesus' spotless robe of righteousness.

While I don't think I'd ever use this poem to teach kids what righteousness is, I do think it's got all the basics. We must remember that it matters whose righteousness we have. We need the righteousness of God (2 Corinthians 5:21); we need HIS RIGHTEOUSNESS! Our goodness won't suffice, but His will!

HIS RIGHTEOUSNESS

That he would clothe me with himself,

His righteousness my only wealth.

To enter through his gates

And seal this happy fate.

Away from God was I

But he came down here to die,

To wear my coat of shame

And to give me his own name.

Why should all my sin be hid

In this precious blood of his?

This is love and grace divine,

No greater love can I find.

That in the eyes of Father God

Should the Son be rejected,

For such a stinking wretch as I

To be in him accepted?

And now this life freely to live,

Not to myself, but unto him.

Free from my wicked deeds of sin,

My holiness is all from him.

And as the risen Savior reigns

So do I trust in his name.

And to the Father he presents

Me in his own righteousness.

And when that day of victory comes

At the setting of the sun,

In Christ alone, shall I be found

Holy and guiltless, all around.

GIVE ME THE CROSS

Give me the cross, say that I'm not lost.

Show me the grave, show that you are raised.

Tell of your life, life that is mine.

Wash out my mind with your Spirit divine.

Help me to yearn for what I can't see.

Show me the hands that were pierced all for me.

CHRIST DIED FOR THE UNGODLY

The punishment taken for me,

The light that made the blind man see,

The gift given to the lowly,

"Christ died for the ungodly."

The mount of sin was trampled down,

When grace came forth with trumpet sound.

The blood that dripped upon the ground,

"Christ died for the ungodly."

He brought the dead man back to life

And truly ended all our strife.

Who was the perfect sacrifice?

"Christ died for the ungodly."

He took our sin upon himself

And bore God's wrath for our own health.

For he could not stand wicked filth,

"Christ died for the ungodly."

He came to save the helpless ones,

To do the work that must be done.

It's finished! Our souls are won!

"Christ died for the ungodly."

And then he rose up from the grave,

Proving that he alone can save.

Will you come to him today

Who died for the ungodly?

POEMS IN AWE OF JESUS

OH, TO SEE THE FACE OF JESUS

Oh, to see the face of Jesus.

Oh, to see God pure and true

Means the end of sin and pure trust in him

And a life anew.

Oh, to bow down to the master.

Oh, to praise him evermore,

Where no stain or guilt will again be spilt,

For our sin he bore.

So until that great day cometh

When our Lord returns again,

We will look to him to be cleaned from sin.

I will follow till the end.

THERE IS NO OTHER POWER I'LL TRUST

There is no other power I'll trust;

There is no one I know

Besides the Lord, my Jesus Christ,

Who saves the sin sick soul.

He came a baby placed in hay,

The King of Kings has come!

Though only dirty shepherds heard

The news the angels rung.

The Son of God became a man,

The perfect took on flesh,

To clothe the sinful evil ones

In his righteousness.

I'll trust nothing but Christ our Lord

Who died and rose again

To reconcile sinful man

Into God's loving hand.

Oh yes, my heart does long for more,

Oh God, fill it with you!

For in my Lord is righteousness

And perfect light so true.

POETIC GLEANINGS ON THE NAME OF JESUS

There is a name like no other,

A name that bids me grace,

A name that is above all else

Of triumph and of faith,

That bids me peace,

That gives me life,

That raises me from the grave.

There is a name above all names,

A name that's to be praised,

A name of mercy,

A name of power,

A name of blessings so.

A name of wondrous, merciful grace

That brightens all my woes.

A name that is above all else.

A name that is so pure,

A name that is above all names

That makes my faith so sure.

Though humbled with a blood-stained brow,

He hung upon a tree;

There he bore the sins of all

Who solely trust in he.

For with the sinless blood, so pure,

He cleanses every stain.

Whose name was scoffed and mocked upon

And beaten down with shame.

Whose name was laughed at like mere jest,

May we tremble at the sound.

Whose name does mean the end of sin,

Eternal life around.

Whose name means healing.

Whose name means peace.

May all men trust in thee,

For at his name all knees will bow

Yes, Jesus, it is he!

POEM ON THE WORD

He is the expressed Word of God
Who spoke all into being,
And by his power sustains all
Of his created beings.

The word of God, incarnate he,
Image of God revealed.
He came down to us humbly
With grace and truth to heal.

In him no lie was ever found;
Indeed, he is The Truth,
The promise from the mouth of God,
The promised Jesse's root.

Whose words could speak life into men
And raise them from the dead.
Who speaks with authority and power,
He is the living bread.

By his command he sets those free

Who hide in slavery,

And declares sinners holy

Before the mercy seat.

He who sustains the universe

Became a man to die,

So that, in him, those far away

Might find in him true life.

MY VEIL WAS LIFTED, NOW I SEE

My veil was lifted
And now I see
The face of Jesus
And his glory!

For when the law
Would condemn me,
My stubborn heart
Refused to see.

But then the Son
Unveiled my face
To now behold
His glorious grace.

And by his Spirit
I am set free,
And now forever
Called holy.

And as I gaze

At his glory,

The Lord my God

Changes me

To make me more like Christ, my King,

This light from God, of whom I'll sing!

SECTION: SIN

Sin is an old-fashioned word, but it's also an important one. Sin is our big problem. It's why everything is so messed up in the world. It's why we are so messed up.

This section seeks to explore the effects and nature of sin. Some of the following poems, such as *Tear down your Idols* have been written out of frustrations over my own struggles, and others, such as *Ensnared in Darkness* I have written in response to our messed-up culture. You don't have to be a Christian to understand that the world is a lost, hurting, and broken place. And I'm sure I am not the only person reading this book who often becomes anguished in some way, shape, or form over sin.

If you don't ever feel convicted over sin, then you really don't understand how damning sin really is. Sin is an offense to God. It is not loving God with your whole heart and not loving your neighbors as yourself (Matthew 22:36-

40); sin is rebellion against God. It's spitting in the face of the Holy One. It breaks our relationships not only here on earth, but also with God in heaven. Sin is the opposite of good. Sin is evil and the Bible teaches that all have sinned (Romans 3:23) and that the result is not only death, but eternal death in Hell.

I am assuming that many who are reading this are Christians and believe that you are saved not only from Hell, but also from sin. If you are saved, then you can be certain that's true. But this does not mean that we still don't sin. The Bible teaches us that we are all going through a process of sanctification; we are being made more like Jesus Christ. Much like the Apostle Paul we find ourselves doing things we later wished we didn't, or even willfully rejecting God (Romans 7:15-23). But Paul is not quick to defeat; rather, by God's grace in him, he strives all the more to grow in obedience towards Jesus Christ (Romans 7:16-26).

All of this is to say that we need to stop hiding behind our picture-perfect Christian profiles and acting like we are better than everyone else. We can't keep deceiving ourselves that the Christian life is an easy task. No, the Christian life is hard. It's a constant war against sin. It's saying no to ungodliness and confessing our sins to each other. We need to meet with each other and be vulnerable, admitting that we've got more issues than we want to admit. We must not give up! Nor must we rely upon our own strength. For no mere man can ever defeat sin… but the God-Man can. His Spirit is within us. May we say with the Apostle Paul, *"Wretched man that I am! Who will deliver me from this body of death? Thanks be to God through Jesus Christ our Lord!"* (Romans 7:24-25)

INTRODUCTION:

WHAT I AM IN CHRIST, I AM NOT. SO I SAY:

I wanted to add this poem because it's one of those "real life" poems, and I'd be willing to bet I'm not the only one with these thoughts. This is not a theology poem. This poem questions a lot of God's promises. In essence this is a poetic prayer of complaint. God has promised to sanctify us (John 17:16) and has called us a new creation (2 Corinthians 5:17) yet all too often I feel like I'm either going back to the same kinds of sin or finding new ones that weigh me down and suck the joy out of my life. My heart was in anguish as I wrote this poem… but I really like the ending. God is still at work in me, and, if he is your savior, he's at work in you too!

73

WHAT I AM IN CHRIST, I AM NOT. SO I SAY.

Where did the fellowship go?

Where are the happy faces?

Why don't people ask how I am?

I'm dying on the inside

And nobody knows.

Well, except the Great I Am.

But here I stand in my filth,

Rebelling against him.

Prayer in the morning, sinning at noon,

I shove his word into my head,

But still I feel dead.

The glory I beheld, I see no more.

What I am in Christ, I am not,

So I say.

He calls me to himself, and I run the other way.

He tells me "come here," and all I do is stay.

He softens his voice, but I won't listen today.

Now I'm hopeless and lonely.

I used to say "hi" to everyone I meet;

Now I just pass on the other side of the street.

I used to be cheery, but now it's all gloom.

Surely, I have planned my own doom.

Every day goes by, my mind is torn in two.

God vs. Me, what should I do?

Why do all these battles end up where they began,

Stuck in sin and hiding from man.

You say I'm alive; I feel dead.

You carry my burdens, but I carry a heavy head.

You are light; but the world around me is dark.

Your love is pure, but my mind is torn apart.

If you planned to clean me, why am I still dirty?

This body of sin, dying day by day,

And here I thought that you were The Way.

But where shall I go? Shall I go to what I hate?

The sin in my heart, that Wretched Fate?

Who, but the Christ, has eternal life?

And, so, with a weakening voice

I faintly cry out this noise.

"Save me, Jesus,

Though I doubt with sinful strife

You listen even now after all my spite.

And so humbly I bow,

Please, help me, Lord, please do.

Right now I do not want to be like you, but…

I want to want to be like you."

BACKSLIDE

I fear that I may backslide
And say I never knew
The one who died and rose again
To make me someone new.
I fear the crowds will mock him,
"Crucify the Lord!"
And I'll give into pressure
And do it all the more.

I know that I'm not of the world.
I know that I am saved,
But still I fear that dreadful thought
That I could run away.
I believe in perseverance,
His sanctifying power,
And, yet, I fear that I should fall
To the world's persuasive power.

Oh, Lord, help me stand steadfast,

Unwavering in faith;

Don't let me try to free myself

From your unyielding grace.

Deal with me as your student,

And help me to believe

My faith rests not in my own hands,

But in God who upholds me.

But still I pray, "Lord help me;

Don't let me give in.

Help me to stay close by you

And let your promise win."

INTRODUCTION:
TEAR DOWN YOUR IDOLS

When we think of the word "idol," we typically think of engravings of wood and stones that people set up and bow down to as if they were gods. Many people today strongly believe that these engravings are gods, but the word idol has taken on more meaning than just this. Take for instance, *American Idol*, which is a show that's all about finding the best and then putting the best above the rest. Though *American Idol* is a show about singing, there is a lesson to be learned here.

Believe it or not, we were created to worship. We were created to put God above everything else. Yet, often we find ourselves bowing to all sorts of idols, and I'm not just talking about other religions. When we put our family, our friends, our stuff, or even ourselves above God, we've made an idol (Exodus 20:3-6). We've persuaded ourselves that there is something more beautiful and good than our all-perfect God. But, inevitably, misplaced things, no matter how good make terrible gods. Idols consume us (Psalm 135:15-18). That's what *Tear Down Your Idols* is ultimately about, finding the false gods in our lives, putting them back into their proper places, and worshiping the true God once again. Worship God, keep yourselves from idols (1 John 5:21).

TEAR DOWN YOUR IDOLS

Some of them walk,

Some of them breathe,

Some are ideas in my head.

Few are evil,

Most are good,

Yet weigh on me like lead.

Some I make,

Some I have,

Some I just desire.

Yet all of them

Have taken the place

Of the One who is higher.

Man, tear down your idols.

Let them all fall down.

Dare not run to them again,

For you stand on Holy Ground.

Sometimes I run

to them so

And pursue with all my power;

Sometimes I run

Away from them

And from the idol cower.

My heart is torn,

It's ripped apart

Between my God and things.

It's far too hard

To let them go,

And all to Christ now cling.

I worship me,

I worship stuff,

I worship people too.

Appreciation,

Love of self,

I don't know what to do.

I was made

To serve my God,

Yet often I'm a slave.

I was freed

To worship him,

Yet still, my idols stay.

I want to live

For God alone;

Yet I wander away.

Oh Lord, my God

Please bring me back;

Help me not to go astray.

Man, tear down your idols,

Let them all fall down.

Dare not run to them again,

For you stand on Holy Ground.

I knock them down,

But every time

They seem to rise again.

I wish to see

The day that all

My idolatry will end.

Yet I hold hope,

For God's at work

In my heart every day,

Turning me

With discipline,

That I may walk his way.

And I am certain

That in the end

My idols all will fall.

When I behold

Jesus' face,

I'll have unending awe.

He'll tear down my idols

And with them replace

True worship to God, my King

As I stand amongst his grace.

WHERE IS MY GOD?

I wander and weave away from your word,

Till then, at last, your voice is not heard.

And then I call out; I ask where you are,

Blaming you for having gone, oh so far.

I open the book with glazed-over eyes,

Not with much joy or even a cry.

I lie on my bed to rest my small head,

Forgetting the words that I should have read.

I look to mere pleasure; I look to mere fun:

I look to be busy and get the job done.

I look far away and look very near,

But where is my God, who my course should steer?

I delight in sin, ignoring him so,

And wallow in guilt, in anger and woe.

But where is my God who has helped me? Oh!

Where could he be; oh where did he go?

How could my God leave a saint that he loved,

One he made holy, decreed from above?

Why can't I see him, why am I blind;

When his Holy Spirit has opened my eyes?

Bring me back in, your prodigal son,

Your treasure, your joy, this wretch you have won,

And help me to love you and turn once again

To my dear God, who has called me his friend.

TREASURES

The world has wrapped around me,

Its treasures fill my eyes;

Such treasures all shall perish,

Consumed by rust and flies.

Yet still they're so enchanting,

Yet still there's much to gain.

Would I gain the whole world

And have my eye be maimed?

The eye is never satisfied,

The ear is never filled,

Every new thing I desire

Will leave me unfulfilled.

Everything is vanity

All is but the wind,

What can treasure offer

When this short life is dimmed?

The Lord provided all good things;

Need I any more?

You can't love God and money,

One master and no more.

So why am I so worried

And want such endless gold?

For God does give me life and breath,

A grace kindly bestowed.

INTRODUCTION:
LADY LUST

I find that many Christians, both male and female, struggle with lust in some way. Some use their imagination to play out sexy scenes in their minds, while others are drawn to books and movies that include half-naked men or women; many watch pornography and can't seem to escape it, some chase after people of the same gender, and still others have had sex before or perhaps even during marriage with someone to whom they are not married. We have a sex crazed culture and it has infiltrated the Church.

There are many in the church who try not to talk about such issues. To some, sex seems like a three-letter curse word, and, to others, it seems, as some song writers put it, like "heaven on earth." But sex is a reality, and according to the Bible is a good thing that has its place inside of a God-ordained marriage between one man and one woman. In fact, the Bible includes a whole book about marriage and sexual desire called *The Song of Solomon,* but it also warns us against giving in to that desire in a wrong way. The following poem is heavily inspired by Proverbs 7, which shows the danger of lustful desires.

Proverbs 7 was not written to unbelievers, but to believers. Therefore, we can assume that God knows we will be tempted by such things. It shows the adulterous woman, "Lady Lust" as she woos an unsuspecting victim into her clutches. The man sought excitement and life, but he soon found that he was in for more than he bargained. Lust is a stupid thing, wisdom less and selfish, which is quite different than love, which according to 1 Peter 3:7 shows value and cherishes others as "co-heirs" in Christ. No matter what your relationship status is, choose love, not lust.

LADY LUST

I stood at the door of Lady Lust;
Her eyes pierced through the window.
The choice was now mine to enter in.
Shall I listen to her lingo?

Yet I heard of men who walked in there,
Though they know they shan't,
To meet that lady's open arms,
The one of whom men chant.

They said she'd give him quite a thrill;
They said that she was kind;
They claimed her as a goddess
Like Aphrodite divine.

So in he walked his conscience seared,
And there he met her eyes;
Her gaze was meant to draw him in,
But he felt like he died.

She sat him on her couch that day.

She said, "Don't make a scene."

She bathed then for ten hours, they say,

Her sin so soft and clean.

She broke some bread and poured some wine

And said that all was well;

Yet still somehow he felt as though

He just stepped into Hell.

As she held the bread she broke,

"Remember me," she said.

"I will give you pure delight.

Yes, I'll stay inside your head."

He ate and drank full of delight,

And then, when night time came,

She opened the bed curtain

And welcomed him to shame.

The bed was laid with purple silk
Like ages long ago.
And, when he sat beside her there,
He knew he had to go!

He told her "No! I've had enough!"
He told her, "I can't stay!
Wisdom calls within the fog.
I'll live another day!"

But to her that mighty man fell.
He tasted false delight,
And with Lady Lust's dreadful bite
Death became his night.

Still my mind stands at the door.
Should I enter in?
Should I take delight in her,
And do this grievous sin?

Lady Lust calls out to me

But so does Wisdom, too;

And by God's grace I'll turn away.

Wisdom I will pursue!

OH, THE DAY WHEN ALL SIN IS NO MORE

All I want is to be

Free from this misery

And to see that glassy sea

Not far away.

All I want is for you

To make me more like you

And to walk in your way every day.

Oh, the day when all sin is no more.

Oh, the day when the city of God is before

The eyes of this man of dust.

All I want is to be

Ever free from sin.

All I want

Is to turn from evil.

All I want is for you,

My Father and Friend,

To overcome every struggle.

Oh, the day when all sin is no more.

Oh, the day when the city of God is before

The eyes of this man of dust.

All I want is to stand

As I am in Jesus,

Free from all sin

And vice.

And I have this pure hope

That is brighter than light,

That from sin I'll be finally torn.

Oh, the day when all sin is no more.

Oh, the day when the Son of God is before

The eyes of this saint who was saved from sin

And to hear him say, "Enter in."

MASTER OF KINDNESS

Master of kindness, who came here to serve,

How I have wandered, oh how I have swerved.

You bent down low to wash dirty feet.

Why don't I follow and do as you speak?

All loving savior, who died for me,

Why is it so hard for me to see

That you have given your life for me

That I might be free and be totally clean?

My Holy Judge, who watches me so,

Where I may wander you always know.

If I am so stubborn and your Spirit quench

In your pursuit, please do not relent.

YET HE LOVES ME SO!

I don't see why God should love

A sinful child like me,

Spitting in his face,

Sending Christ to Calvary.

A rebel to his will

Who speared and marred his side,

Yet, he says he loves me so

To my great surprise.

But I've been so unholy,

I've been so profane,

In anger thinking curses,

Irreverent to his name.

I want gifts, not the giver,

What good was there to save?

There was no good within me,

But he loved me anyways.

Why should he love me dearly,

When I just run away?

Why should he die for sinners,

When he's perfect in every way?

What gain could he get from me?

None, I am so sure.

Yet he still says he loves me

And died as my sin's cure.

Thank you, Jesus, my savior,

For this I don't deserve,

That you would pull me to yourself

And love me more and more!

GIVE US GRACE

My passions hardly change
As violent as a drug,
And, though my life is new,
I feel far from your love.
Lord, don't let me grow weary.
I know that I am free,
Yet, my heart still wanders,
So keep my mind on thee.

We hunger and we thirst
And often feel alone,
And though we want control,
We need you on our throne.
Lord, don't let us stray from you,
For we are in your fold.
Forgive us of our sins
And let our love be bold.

LORD, give us grace; show us your face.

Give us your love from up above.

You died so that we'd live, and rose up from the grave,

And with that same power our lives you do change.

You make our lives anew

And sanctify us through;

We feast upon your word

And pray that we are heard.

We know you hear us clearly,

But sin makes us to fear;

Yet, as we look to you,

We know that you are near.

You came down to this earth

To make the dead men live.

Though he tries to shame us,

The Devil cannot win.

For in the shadow of the cross

You see us now as clean,

So that we can know you

And in your eyes be seen.

LORD, give us grace; show us your face.

Give us your love from up above.

You died so that we'd live, and rose up from the grave,

And with that same power our lives you do change

Give us your grace, LORD, oh give us grace!

You give us grace, LORD, you give us grace!

SECTION: HOPE AND LONGING

"As the deer pants for streams of water, so my soul pants for you, my God. My soul thirsts for God, for the living God. When can I go and meet with God?" (Psalm 42:1-2). Much of the Christian life is one of longing - longing for the end of sin and a deeper and more intimate relationship with God. We long for the day in which we can see Jesus face to face, and we groan as we wait for his coming, knowing that, when he does, we will be perfect and sinless like him and will experience pain no more (Romans 8:19-23).

God often uses sicknesses, physical trials, heartbreaks, and unfulfilled desires to draw us closer to him and to remind us for whom we are really living. I really resonate with a quote that C.S. Lewis, the author of the much-read books, *Chronicles of Narnia*, once said, "If I find in myself a desire which no experience in this world can satisfy, the most probable explanation is that I was made for another world." *

We've been made for another world. A world that is perfect, and a world where we are sinless. A world without pain… and most importantly, a world lit by the presence of God (Revelation 21:23-25). We long for another world. And when we are saddened that the things of this world can never ultimately fulfill us, we must, as the Psalmist says, "put your hope in God" and remember him (Psalm 42:5-6).

So, the poems in this section are ones of remembrance and longing. It's holding onto hope when your forgetful mind somehow convinces you there is none. And not only that, it is putting your faith in a God you can't always see and saying, "I will trust in you. I will hope in you, despite the doubts and despite the circumstances." These poems are the outcry of my heart, and I hope in times of longing they might remind you to look to God as well and trust in his good name.

105

* Lewis, C. S.. Mere Christianity (C.S. Lewis Signature Classics) (pp. 136-137).

HarperOne. Kindle Edition..

INTRODUCTION:

EVERY LONGING OF MINE

Everyone longs for something. Though many religions tell us to ignore our desires, biblical Christianity does not. Rather, we are to give our desire to God, saying, "if the Lord wills I will do this or that" (James 4:13-15). We have hearts that were made to desire. When we long for sin, we must confess it to Jesus and seek better things. Yet still sometimes we feel like God is ignoring our longings for good things: "Why don't I have a better job?" "Why must I go through all this suffering?" "Why can't I understand my math homework?" The list could go on, but, even when we don't seem to have our longings fulfilled, we must remember that in the end... Jesus is, and will always be enough.

EVERY LONGING OF MINE

Every longing of mine,

Every want and desire,

Every thought, every will,

Everything I aspire,

Is met in Thee,

The God of Heaven

Who gives and takes

And does what you may

To draw me nearer

To the water that satisfies.

Every vain desire,

Every evil want,

Every sin, and every deed,

Everything against your will

Is lack compared

To the immeasurable pleasure

That comes from Jesus,

Who fills our hunger

With the bread from heaven.

Every loving want,

Every good desire,

Every wish, every need,

Every gift that I ask for,

Even if they never come,

Even if you deny my basic needs,

Yet still my treasure and portion are Thee;

And one day, You I will see!

Every thought and every love,

Every path I take,

Ever yearning, ever desiring,

Let me with Thy help aspire

To run for you above all else,

To give my life to long for you

Who did save me

And will raise me from the grave

To be ever amazed by you.

Amen

WHEN MY HEART FEELS GLOOMY

When my heart feels gloomy,

When my mind feels sad,

I will look to Jesus;

May he make me glad.

When my mind feels lonely,

When my face is down,

May I trust in Jesus;

In him may hope be found.

Though life be a burden,

Though time soon flies by,

May my Lord establish me

And keep me by his side.

And if sin tries to enter,

Do not let it in;

For I'm a new creation,

For I will trust in him.

Clad in all his splendor,

Dressed in righteousness,

In him I am guiltless,

He is my defense.

Though the flesh may mock me

And lead me to the grave,

To that old man I have died,

The Spirit calls me saved.

In him I do find justice,

And in him I find grace.

Never shall he leave me.

Yes, I will see his face!

Though joy, I cannot feel it.

I know in Christ it's found,

So I'll hold to his promise

Until that trumpet sound.

GLEANINGS ON SADNESS

Sometimes the loudest people are actually the quietest.

Sometimes the one who has it all together, does not.

Sometimes the happiest people are those who experience sadness.

Yet all the time God hears, and listens, and loves.

WHATEVER GAIN THIS WORLD MAY HAVE

Whatever gain this world may have,

I lay it down for thee.

Whatever power I might taste

Shall never satisfy me.

If I could sit upon a throne,

If I could rule the earth,

Whatever gain I might have had,

It all is loss for me.

Whatever righteousness of mine

Is nothing I could boast,

For the sinfulness of man

Would damn me the utmost.

For only in this grace divine

And through the risen Lord

Can I have true righteousness

And know him and adore.

HAVE FAITH IN THE FAITHFUL

Have faith in the faithful;

Let him be your guide.

Though we see in part,

He is there all the time.

When our faith grows weary,

Let's look up again.

"Lord, help me have faith

to believe you again."

When like the blind man

You stumbled in the dark,

Remember how your Savior

Opened your burdened heart.

Though you see shadows,

And all seems a blur,

He'll touch your eyes again

To see God truer and sure.

Oh! What a sorrow!

Oh! what a shame!

My faith is so weak;

It's so meek and lame!

But Oh, listen Child.

Be not ashamed.

Stand up and have courage,

Because from God it came.

Your faith is not from you;

It comes from God above,

A gift from our Savior

Sent to us with love.

By faith are we saved,

And this is all from God.

So take heart! Stand firm!

Look to our Faithful God!

HOPE REFOCUSED

When hope seems hopeless,

And all seems lost,

Refocus your hope

Back on the Cross.

When hope is deadly

And drives you mad,

Remember him

Who makes you glad.

Some hope is worthless,

Some hope is vain;

But hope in God,

And you'll never be shamed.

Hope in God,

The Three in One.

Hope in the Father who sent his Son.

Hope in the Son who made a way

For the guilty to be saved.

Hope in the Spirit who opened our eyes.

This hope is not hopeless but leads to life!

HOPE IN THE LORD

Why is my soul downcast?

Put your hope in the Lord;

For though all seems as vanity and dull,

In Christ we have much more.

In him we have eternal life

And joy forever more.

He is our hope and life and peace,

So, hope now in the Lord.

THERE IS A CITY, NOT FAR AWAY

There is a city, not far away,
Made by the Hands of God,
Where no sin or vice will stay,
But where all the saints will trod.

There all tears are wiped away,
And no pain there shall be found
In this city, coming near,
In this city, made by God.

Yes, this earth is not my home;
This body is broke and bare,
But when all heaven shall come down,
A perfect earth we'll share.

We will be just like Jesus,
Never to sin as before
For in this city God is there
And is with us evermore.

INTRODUCTION:
CITY MADE BY GOD

I made this one for a Sunday School lesson from Hebrews 11. Hebrews 11 reminds us to be faithful to our ever-faithful God by the example of saints from the past. One of these saints was Abraham, who despite having the promise that God would bring his people into the Promised Land, he never actually saw that promised realized and lived in the land like a foreigner who didn't belong. The author of Hebrew mentions that "he was looking forward to the city that has foundations, whose designer and builder is God." (Hebrews 11:10). Abraham had a hope that was beyond his own death and that he was certain he would see.

And don't you dare say that Abraham was thinking about Heaven and not a literal city. One of the greatest misconceptions in the church is that we will live forever in some sort of heavenly, disembodied state. That is unbiblical and flies in the face of the greater story of scripture! From the very beginning God made man and woman as both spiritual and physical beings. Death is a separation of those two aspects and is not what God intended. The best news is that, just as Jesus rose from the dead, so will we! Go read 1 Corinthians 15 if you don't agree. Not only that, but the grand story of the Bible ends with all of God's people gathered in a city where sin and death are no more (Revelation 21-22:5). This is our ultimate hope in Jesus! Jesus didn't just save us so that we can be saved and have our sins forgiven only. He saved us to redeem every part of us! God will complete his work, and that heavenly, earthbound city of perfection ought to be a part of our hope! So, may we live like Abraham in our present cities, towns, and country sides, knowing that we, too, are foreigners and awaiting that promised city from God.

CITY MADE BY GOD

Shall I long for all the power

That this earth could ever share?

Shall I seek for myself

All the riches I could bear?

Or shall I wait, and shall I walk

As a Stranger in this land,

Waiting for the great reward,

A place made by God's own hand?

Shall I love and wallow in

All the evil deeds of man?

Shall I walk in wicked pleasures,

Acting as if I were damned?

Or shall I fight, and shall I live

As my Savior did?

Knowing that there'll be no sin

In the city made by God.

Shall I forge with all my might

My own page in history?

Shall I glory in my name,

Praise and honor all to me?

Or shall I now with all my heart

Glorify his name,

With all hope prepare to sing

In a city made by God?

Shall I stumble in the darkness

Of this world of sin and pain?

Shall I now, with all despair

Wallowing in its wicked shame?

Or shall I look beyond the night

To the light that comes from God

And await that joyful sight

In the city made by God.

Yes, I'll await that promised city

Where all His people are called Holy,

Though I never should be there.

In this promise, I will share,

For my God is true and faithful

And his promises are sure.

And if time seems long and weary,

I will wait upon the LORD.

SECTION: LIFE OF WORSHIP

When one becomes a Christian, there is a life of worship ahead of him or her. Those who think that Christianity is merely a get-out-of-Hell-free scheme are wrongly mistaken. The Bible, rather, calls us to a joyful service of Christ. These poems seek to give a glimpse of how that looks. For instance, the poem "WE" emphasizes the unity of believers. Our culture is very individualistic, but in Christ we are called to bear with one another and forgive them as Christ has forgiven us (Ephesians 4:32). We are not called in Christ towards individualism, but towards unity and community.

In addition, we are called to be conformed to Christ, which means we are to be made more into his image. We are to walk like him, talk like him, and show his love in everything that we do. Many times, that includes suffering, but, when suffering comes, we can still look to Christ knowing that he is wisely conforming us to himself and gives

us the power to persevere through trials.

A LOVE THAT REACHES

A love that reaches.

A love that cares.

A love that I just want to share.

The love of Jesus.

A love that's mine.

Please, oh Lord, let your love shine.

WORTHSHIP

As we gaze upon the cross of Christ

Once again, we see

The worthship of the king of kings

Who died for you and me.

So let us come to worship now

And pray unto the Lord.

Help us worship; show us how.

Your Word let us adore!

"WE"

We will go where you take us.

We will stay where you stay.

We will show the love of Jesus,

We will follow in your way.

For in love you laid your life down,

And for us you were slain.

For you rose and gave your Spirit,

So that we may do the same.

WE LIVE

We live because he lives in us.
We live for we are free.
We live because he died for us
Upon that cursed tree.

For we are free from every sin
That held us in the grave;
For by his resurrected power
We're sanctified today.

We live to love; we live to serve,
Not to be slaves to sin,
To worship him in every hour
Forever to praise him.

We live because he rose again;
We know that we will too,
For death is dead in Jesus Christ
And life is sure and true.

JOY AMIDST THE FLAMES

Through every trial I shall go,

This Lord let me know,

Though in the fire I may be,

You refine me so.

Give me joy amidst the flames,

For this is not in vain,

To grow my faith and help me stand

Steadfast by your name.

And though these trials may bring pain,

Let me trust in You.

For I shall be made more like him,

Whose perfect, pure, and true.

And from the furnace I shall come

Refined and bright like gold,

Standing firm against the world

That seeks to wreck my soul.

So now I praise and sing to thee,

For finally I see

My God has been so kind to me,

Though he's been testing me.

For though the earth may quake with fear,

My faith will never turn,

For he will make me grow in faith,

So that it's strong and firm.

And so I sing unto my Lord,

Give me now such joy

As I persevere and stand

By the strength that you employ!

MAY I TAKE UP MY CROSS AND FOLLOW THEE

May I take up my cross and follow Thee,

Who bore all my burdens on Calvary's tree.

May I cast all my cares fully on Thee,

As I follow you in the way.

Let me love God whole-heartedly.

Let nothing else come before thee,

Rather, let me eagerly

Bear the cross with thee.

Do not let my life be wasted so

In a life of vain pleasure,

But let all my longing be to

Follow you day by day.

I find it odd that, as I walk,

this cross doesn't seem so heavy.

But then I looked up and saw him there,

He who bore all my sin for me.

Whatever may come both good or bad

May I now be eternally glad,

For he took my cross upon himself

To give me true life and eternal wealth.

LORD, I AM YOUR SERVENT

Lord, I am your servant,

Freed to serve you.

A slave to sin no longer,

Now God I'll pursue.

And what a loving Master,

The lowly Righteous King,

May I always trust in you

And of your goodness sing.

Oh, that I'd always love you

And with my soul pursue

To love my savior and my King

Jesus through and through.

INTRODUCTION:
STOP WAITING, SINGLE SOUL:

There are a lot of single people in the church and I find that many of them become very discouraged. Why hasn't God given me "the one" yet? Doesn't anybody love me? What's wrong? These are typically unasked questions and unfortunately the only answer people seem to give is to either "wait" or to "date around."

My friend Tirus once preached a sermon called "Marriage or Singleness: Which is the Ultimate?" in a student-run preaching group at LBC. He had recently gotten married and wanted to preach a sermon to encourage the singles in the group (which were most of us). So, which was the ultimate? His verdict came from 1 Corinthians 7. Neither! He reminded us that the ultimate was "undivided devotion to the Lord." A married man or woman can serve by serving his or her spouse, although it might be a bit easier for a single man or woman to do more.

At the time of writing this, I am still single. I'm only in my 20's now, so I guess it's not that big of a deal. Many days I really do enjoy being single, but other days I just want to find "the one." I think that is a sentiment many other Bible college students understand. One thing I've learned over the years is to see this part of my life not as a waiting period but as an opportunity from God for focused service to him. I've had more time on my hands to do more, to reach the lost, and to encourage others more than I would had had if I had been dating someone. Biblical singleness is not a call to laziness, but to happily serve God's church.

I really do hope to make and publish a poem like this on marriage one day, but I've decided not to until I've experienced marriage myself. So sorry, married friends, you'll have to wait (Ephesians 5:21-33 will DEFINITELY be my inspiration). But don't think that being married means you don't get to serve God as well. No, both the married and the single will love and serve God and others, but often in different ways. So be encouraged, my friends, and remember who you're ultimately here for!

STOP WAITING SINGLE SOUL

After so much waiting

You'd think you'd find the one;

And every time you hope,

You find your hope undone.

Where is your strong help?

Or where's your leading head,

The one on whom you thought you'd rest your weary head?

You pace back and forth,

Uncertain and unsure.

You wonder what's wrong;

Doesn't God promise much more?

How much more waiting

Until you find the one?

When will all this waiting be done?

Stop waiting, single soul;

Go and serve the bride of Christ,

For you are one with him,

Bought with a mighty price.

Let God be your treasure;

Rest in his gracious hand,

For you were made for him, and in him you stand.

So why don't we take action

And lift our weary heads

Like Paul of Tarsus,

Going wherever we are led?

If we do need another,

He'll provide in time,

Still showing us to trust him in every uphill climb.

Don't think that you're alone,

For God's people are around.

Go serve them as Christ

Would serve his church, his crown.

Let your feet take action;

Let your voice sing high;

And to all those around you

Your savior magnify.

Stop waiting, single soul;

Go and serve the bride of Christ,

For you are one with him,

Bought with a mighty price.

Let God be your treasure;

Rest in his gracious hand,

For you were made for him, and in him you stand.

So, while you wait, get going.

Be open to God's plan.

Don't think that you're unwanted,

For God holds you in his hand.

Have faith and pray more to him;

Ask for his eyes everyday.

Though the world may look in pity,

God says, "Nope, they're mine today!"

Stop waiting, single soul;

Go and serve the bride of Christ,

For you are one with him,

Bought with a mighty price.

Let God be your treasure;

Rest in his gracious hand,

For you were made for him, and in him you stand.

LIKE A TREE, STANDS THE MAN

Like a tree

Stands the man

Who relies upon God's hand!

Every season

Bearing fruit,

Because water runs through his roots.

Wind or storm,

He shall prevail,

Because God keeps him through the hail.

And trust in God,

Yes, he shall do,

And in his shade others will too!

EARS TO LISTEN

Give me ears to listen and eyes to see

The hurting world around me.

Give me love to show and feet to go

To tell the Gospel and Jesus show.

CONFORM ME TO CHRIST

Here I am,

Conform me to Christ;

For he is my life;

Nothing else will suffice.

GIVE THANKS IN ALL THINGS

Give thanks in all things.

Oh, how could I be

Able to give my thanks all to thee?

And how can I stay

Thankful each day,

When my heart is selfish and runs every way?

Give thanks in all things,

In trials, in joys,

In wounds and in worries, in storms and in noise.

Give thanks when all life

Seems to go wrong.

Give thanks to my God with a still joyful song.

Give thanks in all things,

And here we see why.

Give thanks for he draws us near to his side.

Through every hard trial

Or grassy green road,

The Word, our Lord Jesus, is leading us so.

Give thanks in all things,

For through them we see

That all of these trials make us more like He.

Give thanks in your Savior

Who calls you His own,

For we know that our Father will never disown!

DIVINE INTERJECTION

Devoid of joy

Like vain machines

We wallow towards the pews.

With sleepy hearts

And tired hands

We dare not look to you.

The pastor's mouth

And arms move on;

He's studied day and night,

But the people

With interest gone

Peer on with little light.

Yet then, by some

Divine interjection,

An eye is opened wide,

And at the preaching

Of the cross

New passion bubbles inside.

And one by one

By prayer and the Word

The people's ears are pierced.

Their empty jars

Are filled with hope,

Their love is ever fierce.

SECTION: OUR BIG GOD

The Christian God is the biggest God there is, and that's because he is the true God! If God truly is all-powerful and all knowing, why are we thrown through a loop when some things don't make perfect sense.

For instance, the Bible teaches that God is a Trinity. He is one God in three different persons (Deuteronomy 6:4) (Matthew 3:16-17). The Father is not the Son, and the Son is not the Spirit. Three persons in one God. God does not switch modes, nor was the Son created by the Father. All three are eternally existent and eternally one God. Confusing, right? Its okay to scratch your head; we have a big God. Even though the Bible never mentions the word 'Trinity,' its authors are keenly aware that they are teaching about one God in three different persons. Yet it doesn't bother them, because he is God!

Another conundrum comes from how God can be sovereign and still allow people to sin. The Bible pretty much says, "who are we to question God" as an answer (Romans 9:20). While it may seem to be avoiding the question it, actually shows how we cannot fully understand God. Throughout the Bible we see man's free will and God's sovereignty both at work. Somehow God is entirely in control of everything that happens, and man still can make decisions for which he is responsible.

I am from what you might call "the reformed tradition," which means I hold the sovereignty of God to be very important. I believe that our salvation is all from God. Before we were saved, we were utterly evil and did not want God (Romans 3:10-12), but God lovingly and irresistibly drew us to himself to believe in him. I've been brought from death to life (Ephesians 2:1-10). I chose God because he first chose me. What a beautiful mystery. I am grateful for God's sovereign grace, as you might see in the final poem in this section: *A Hymn on God's Choice.*

All of this is to say that we have a great God who is worthy to be worshiped. May the poems in this section remind you of our big God!

TRINITARIAN POETRY JAM

The Father sent his Son,

Who came to die for us.

The Son sent the Spirit,

Who now abides in us.

KING OF KINGS, TO YOU WE SING!

King of Kings, to you we sing,

And to you all praises we bring.

God almighty, Lord of all,

To your feet we fall in awe.

Holy Father, God of all,

On us does your pleasure fall.

For by the blood of Christ the King

Our redemption does he bring.

God made manifest in flesh

To give us wicked men rest,

To abolish sin and death.

In God's Son we make our nest.

God the Spirit, Lord inside,

By you we are sanctified.

In the Son let us abide,

And in you let us always stride.

CREATED BY GOD TO WORSHIP HIM

Created by God to worship his name,

Ordained to give him praise,

With joyful hearts now let us bring

Songs of joy and grace.

Set now your hearts on the Holy One.

Look now and see his love.

Sing anew the love of God,

Who came to earth from above.

Who are we to sing God's praise?

Better the rocks than man!

But in God's preordained plan

He calls us to worship the Lamb.

As we look into your word

And see your righteous love,

Let us together all adore

And worship the Lord from above!

How could mere men sing your praise,

Except by the cross of the King?

And now, O God, we look to you;

Your praises do we sing!

THE POT AND THE CREATOR

I am the pot,

And you are my creator.

I am created,

And you have always been.

Who am I to counsel

You in what to do?

What more could I add

To the Wisdom that's in you?

Forgive me, my God,

For I often ask you why.

Why was I made like this

Or some blessing passed me by?

But who am I to question

You in all your ways?

You're sovereign and you're glorious

Showing mercy every day.

Though your hand's invisible

And I don't see you work,

Help me still to trust you,

The Potter at his work.

And let me thank you more and more

That you would still choose me,

A small and dirt-made jar of clay

To love and show glory.

ALL WILL KNOW THAT YOU ARE GOD

And all will know that you are God
Above all earthly powers,
Who'll crush the wicked in his hands
And open justice's showers.

The nations know that you are God
As the Church still grows,
And as the Lord does work his will
Protecting those he chose.

But when his people turn away,
Though he won't pour out wrath,
He'll discipline them as his sons
And lead them back to his path.

For on the cross he bore our sin;
His wrath is pacified.
But those who are not of his fold
Could never run and hide.

But they still know that he is God,

And he is just and fair;

And those who turn to follow him

Are freed from Hell's despair.

AWAKEN OUR HEARTS

Oh, that you might

awaken our hearts

To the beauty of your Word,

So your power

And sanctifying way

Might be clearly heard.

Let us drink

From the rivers of life,

And towards Jesus let us stare.

And lift up our prayers

With joy and delight,

Knowing that our God does care.

Reveal to us your majesty

And draw our hearts to you.

May we in eager hope

Find delight in you.

Never to seek in vain delights,

But always in your word,

As we look towards your divine glory,

Assured our prayers are heard.

A HYMN ON GOD'S CHOICE

There was nothing good in us,
No works of grace were found;
But in our vain deceitful hearts
Was darkness all around.
Yet God in mercy chose us still
And brought us to his throne,
And in his unsearchable will
He made us his own.

The Father sent the Son to earth
To accomplish his plan
And to redeem from all the earth
A race from sinful man.
Upon that cross, where mercy flowed,
He died for his redeemed
And rose again from death to life;
On Christ alone we lean.

How could we have come to God

Except by his good pleasure?

He drew the rebels to his side

With grace beyond our measure.

His Sprit dragged and pulled us there

And with his divine power

He made in us a heart of flesh

To seek him every hour.

Should we like mortal men despair

And fear that he'll reject us,

If the sovereign God wouldn't spare

The precious blood of Jesus?

He chose us to glorify him

And sealed us with the Spirit,

And by his grace he'll bring us

Into Christ's good appearance.

Who could say this was themselves

And take away the glory?

For we know this all was from God-

His plan, his grace, his story.

We love him for he loved us first,

To God alone the Glory!

For this our purpose and our joy,

To tell of his great story!

SECTION: BONUS FEATURES

So, you've reached the bonus features. This is where I put my "other" poems. I don't have many "other" poems, but I found these fun to write and read.

Winter in the Spring and *I Paint Pictures with My Words* are my attempts at writing a lyrical poem in a similar style as those seen in musicals. Whether or not I actually accomplished that, I'm not sure, but I think they turned out well. But out of all the poems in this section, my favorite one is simply... and aptly named *TACOS*. That poem especially should be a great insight into my cheesy sense of humor. Some may ask why I put a poem about tacos in a book primarily about God... and my reply is simply "because I wanted to." Does God not have a sense of humor? And are not tacos one of his greatest creations on this earth?

In all seriousness, though, I hope you enjoyed this book, *Poems for the Redeemed Heart*. Hopefully it was encouraging to you and somehow lifted your eyes to look at him, Jesus, who has made you and saved you for himself. He loves you so much! Never forget that! If you do not know Jesus as your savior, I hope you will consider following him!

And so, I offer these final few poems in hopes that they will make you smile, as well as a short preview to a novel on which I am currently working and very excited about! The working title of the book is called *Project Green Sword*, and while it has no set release date it has been a passion project of mine for some time! I am not ready to reveal exactly what it will be about just yet but stayed tuned!

Remember, a cheerful heart is good medicine (Proverbs 17:22)!

WINTER IN THE SPRING

It's winter in the spring

And it makes me want to sing

As the gentle snowflakes fall down.

It's winter in the spring,

And oh the joy it brings

As the snow covers the green ground.

Feel the snowflakes fall onto your nose.

Flowers ain't got nothin' on the snow.

And in the darkened light

Still the snow shines bright;

So enjoy it now before it goes.

TACOS

In you I confide;

There's nothing to hide,

For with you I have pure delight.

Your taste is so sweet

Like words from above;

You fill me with grace,

And you fill me with love.

Never again to delight in another,

I'm sold to you, you see.

You might think it's funny, but here's all my money.

Tacos are the food for me.

If I feel sad,

I'll have one or two.

When I eat you,

My fears seem to shoo.

You're beefy inside,

And you're a bit cheesy too,

But there's no other food that I'd rather pursue.

Your shell can be soft

Or can be hard;

It all depends on how I'm feeling.

Inside you are

The choicest delights;

You are a food that's worth stealing. *

You vary from day to day,

And that is ok by me.

Rice, corn, salsa, lettuce.

If it's in the fridge,

That cool pilgrimage,

You'll always be so yummy to me!

*no, I am not advocating taco theft

I PAINT PICTURES WITH MY WORDS

They say a picture's worth a thousand words

With colors bright and swell,

But I paint pictures with my words,

As far as I can tell!

Some will paint them dull and grey

With doom full as the night,

But within every evening sky

There's still a little light.

So put down those tattered brushes,

Hold off that coat of blue,

Just listen close and you will see

What words can do.

Words can say "I Love You,"

Words can show you care.

Take some time to listen

To the voices in the air.

Words can serenade you.

Words can stick around.

Words can cheer you up,

When all you feel is down.

Sometimes there are many words,

And sometimes few are more.

Just to say, "I'll listen,"

Can open mercy's door.

But listen! Take precaution!

Be careful what you say,

Or else you'll cause a friend

To have a very bad, bad day.

Your tongue is like a fire,

So please do use it well

To warm up chilly places,

To build up and make swell.

Look behind the foggy sky,

The water cold midnight,

And wait until the morning star

Comes to give you light.

There's grass beyond the snowy hills,

A place where the sun shines bright;

There's hope that we all need to know,

And words can tell it right.

SNEAK PEAK:
PROJECT GREEN SWORD

"Agape," a soft voice cried through the darkness.

"Agape" it cried again as an unseen figure rolled on his mat.

"Agape," the voice echoed louder. "The Knight comes!"

Agape jumped up with a snap, his dark shadow standing in the pitch-black room. The voice, he thought. It had been so long, but Agape knew who's voice it was.

"What?" Agape said, scratching his head. "What do you mean, 'he comes?'" he said as a green mist began to pour out from the floor throughout the pitch-black room, gently lighting the chubby man's face. His hair was dark black and a bit messy, on his face were two large muttonchops, and his eyes looked into the cloud with wonder. Within the green mist stood a figure, radiant with unspeakable glory. Agape fell to his knees.

"The Knight comes, the day is here." The voice chimed again.

Agape's eyes widened as the green mist sank low to the ground beneath the dimly lit floor boards, leaving him alone standing in the pitch-black room with the purest excitement he could ever fathom.

"The Knight comes!" He exclaimed before the voice could whisper once again.

"The Knight comes."

ABOUT THE AUTHOR

At the time of writing, Kenny A. Bechtel is currently a senior in the Pastoral Ministry department at Lancaster Bible College. The role of a Pastor, though, is not one he believes he is called to. What exactly is Kenny called to? Who knows? He certainly does not! But what he does know is that he desires to use the gift of teaching the Bible, as well as his love for creativity, writing, and fiction to glorify God.

When he isn't writing, Kenny loves to hang out with friends, watch movies (especially *Star Wars*), listen to audiobooks, and do other nerdy things like reading comic books or playing video games!

Also, he really loves writing about himself in the third person... I should probably stop now.

I hope you all enjoyed this book! For more reading both edifying and fun visit my blog at Storybunk.com! Hope to see you there!

www.ingramcontent.com/pod-product-compliance
Lightning Source LLC
Chambersburg PA
CBHW051725040426
42447CB00008B/989